FLOATING IN SPACE

by Franklyn M. Branley • illustrated by True Kelley

HarperCollinsPublishers

Special thanks to Audrey Schwartz
at the Johnson Space Center
for her time and expert review.

The illustrations in this book were done in watercolor and pen and ink on Fabriano watercolor paper.

The *Let's-Read-and-Find-Out Science* book series was originated by Dr. Franklyn M. Branley, Astronomer Emeritus and former Chairman of the American Museum–Hayden Planetarium, and was formerly co-edited by him and Dr. Roma Gans, Professor Emeritus of Childhood Education, Teachers College, Columbia University. Text and illustrations for each of the books in the series are checked for accuracy by an expert in the relevant field. For a complete catalog of Let's-Read-and-Find-Out Science books, write to HarperCollins Children's Books, 10 East 53rd Street, New York, NY 10022, or visit our web site at http://www.harperchildrens.com.

HarperCollins®, ✿®, and Let's Read-and-Find-Out Science® are registered trademarks of HarperCollins Publishers Inc.

FLOATING IN SPACE
Text copyright © 1998 by Franklyn M. Branley
Illustrations copyright © 1998 by True Kelley
Printed in the United States of America. All rights reserved.

Library of Congress Cataloging-in-Publication Data
Branley, Franklyn M. (Franklyn Mansfield), date
  Floating in space / by Franklyn M. Branley ; illustrated by True Kelley.
    p.   cm. — (Let's-read-and-find-out science.   Stage 2)
  Summary: Examines life aboard a space shuttle, describing how astro-
nauts deal with weightlessness, how they eat and exercise, some of the
work they do, and more.
  ISBN 0-06-025432-7. — ISBN 0-06-025433-5 (lib. bdg.)
  ISBN 0-06445142-9 (pbk.)
  1. Life support systems (Space environment)—Juvenile literature.
2. Weightlessness—Juvenile literature.   3. Space shuttles—Juvenile literature. [1. Astronauts.   2. Space Shuttles.]   I. Kelley, True, ill.
II. Title.   III. Series.
TL1500.B73   1998   97-13052
629.47'7—dc21   CIP
                                                                AC

1 2 3 4 5 6 7 8 9 10
❖
First Edition

Jump up. Jump as high as you can. You can't go very high, because Earth's gravity pulls you down. On Earth gravity is strong because Earth contains a lot of material—rocks and soil, water, and metals.

If you were on the moon, you could jump much higher.

The moon's gravity is much weaker than Earth's gravity.

That's because the moon contains much less material.

If you were on a shuttle or a space station, you could jump so high, you would float to the ceiling. Then you would float to the floor.

Up you would float again; up and down, up and down. You would be floating in space. That's because gravity in a shuttle is very weak.

In the shuttle there is so little gravity, it is often called zero gravity. There is no "down" or "up." Astronauts do not jump inside a shuttle or a space station. They move very carefully. They hold on to straps with their hands or their feet. If they keep very still, astronauts can stay wherever they are, even without a strap. But if they lift an arm or a leg, they start moving. They might hit a ceiling or a wall, or they might spin around. Wherever they land, they can stand. That means they could stand on a wall or on the ceiling. Imagine how that would make you feel.

Here on Earth astronauts are used to standing on the floor, just as you and I are. When they first find themselves standing on a wall, many astronauts feel a bit dizzy. But after three or four days most astronauts get used to space, and they enjoy standing on a wall, or even a ceiling.

GRAVITY
50 lbs.

In the shuttle or in a space station you don't feel any weight. You are weightless. Your weight on Earth is the amount of gravity pulling you down. If you weigh fifty pounds, the force of gravity on you is fifty pounds. The heavier you are, the greater the force of gravity on you.

In the shuttle there is very little gravity, almost zero. So there is very little weight, close to zero. That's why it is easy to move. Also, it is easy to lift things, even if they would weigh a ton or more on Earth.

It's really too easy to move around in the shuttle. You hardly need your muscles at all, and you hardly need your bones. But to stay healthy, each of us must use our muscles every day. Astronauts do this by using exercise machines. Even so, when astronauts stay in space very long, their muscles and bones get weaker. And astronauts grow one or two inches taller because gravity isn't pulling on them. When the astronauts return to Earth, they slowly become shorter again. These changes cause backaches for many astronauts.

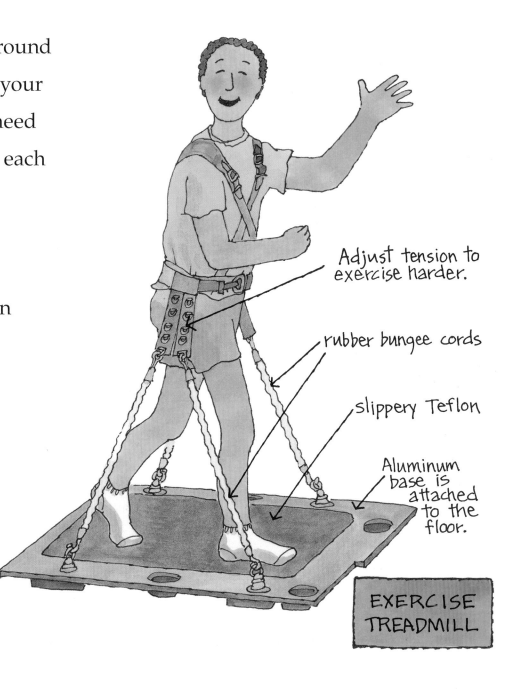

Adjust tension to exercise harder.

rubber bungee cords

slippery Teflon

Aluminum base is attached to the floor.

EXERCISE TREADMILL

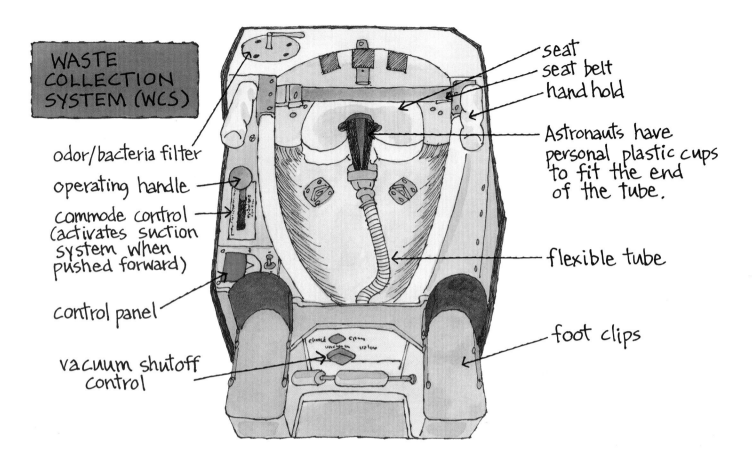

WASTE COLLECTION SYSTEM (WCS)

seat
seat belt
hand hold

Astronauts have personal plastic cups to fit the end of the tube.

odor/bacteria filter

operating handle

commode control (activates suction system when pushed forward)

control panel

vacuum shutoff control

flexible tube

foot clips

Since there is no "down" in space, water cannot flow. That means drinking is through a straw. And using the toilet is somewhat different. The astronaut is strapped to the toilet to keep from floating free. Urine is collected and vented into space. Solid waste is dried and stored until the shuttle lands. The toilet looks and works much like one on an airplane.

DINNER MENU
- shrimp cocktail
- spaghetti with meatless sauce
- peas with butter sauce
- canned peaches
- nuts
- orange drink

straw

Magnetized tray holds utensils in place.

THE GALLEY

food packages oven

trays attached to metal strips on doors

water injector

Tray has magnets and velcro strips underneath so it can be attached to the table or even the wall!

Some of the food astronauts eat is dried. The astronauts mix these foods with water and then heat them in a microwave oven. They often eat food with thick sauces that help the food cling to the tray.

Mealtime aboard is often playtime. Astronauts might float a piece of candy and then try to catch it in their mouths. A favorite trick is to suspend a big drop of fruit drink and then slurp it up with a straw. Salt and pepper are in liquid form so crystals do not float around the cabin. Eating in space takes practice!

All the food for the astronauts must be carried aboard the shuttle. But water is given off by the shuttle's fuel cells as they make electricity. The water is collected and then used for cooking, drinking, and washing.

Tanks of air are also carried aboard, because there is no air in space. The inside of the shuttle is filled with air, so the astronauts can breathe. Outside the ship there is no air, so astronauts must wear space suits, and breathe air from tanks that they carry with them.

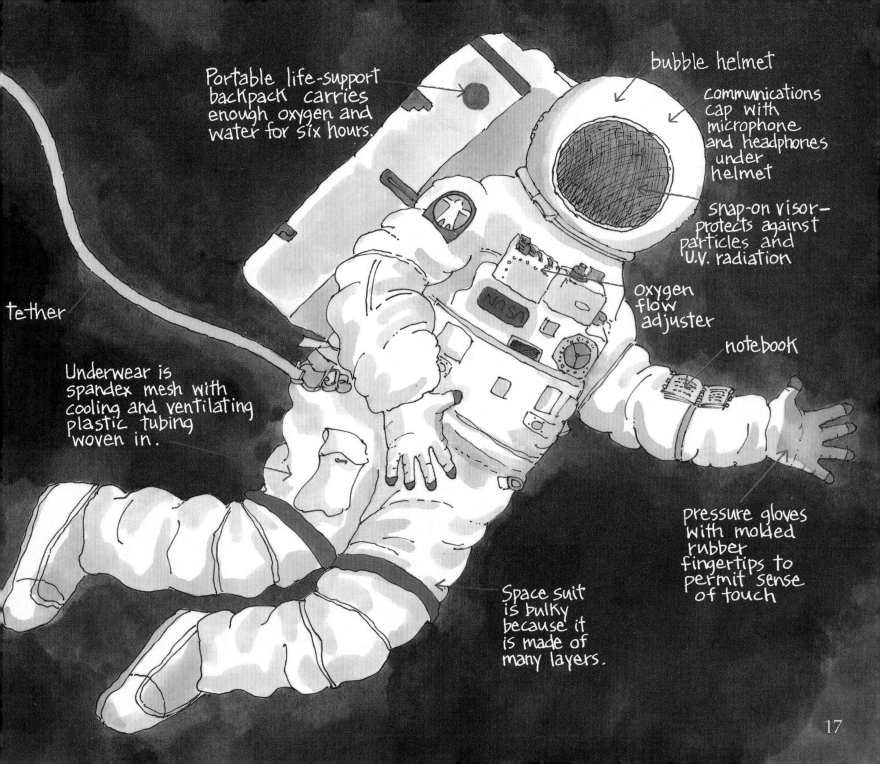

Portable life-support backpack carries enough oxygen and water for six hours.

bubble helmet

communications cap with microphone and headphones under helmet

snap-on visor—protects against particles and U.V. radiation

tether

Oxygen flow adjuster

notebook

Underwear is spandex mesh with cooling and ventilating plastic tubing woven in.

NASA

pressure gloves with molded rubber fingertips to permit sense of touch

Space suit is bulky because it is made of many layers.

17

SUITING UP

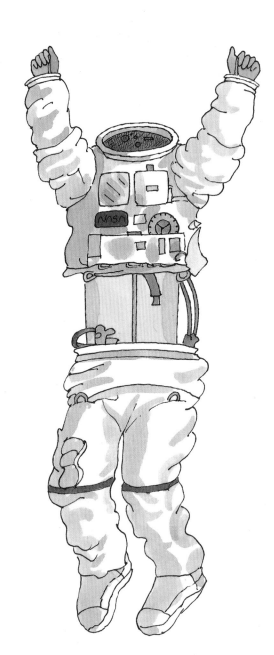

The suits are big and clumsy, and it is hard for astronauts to move about when they wear them. But they can do hard jobs. They have fixed big satellites and put them back into orbit. They are building a space station for the twenty-first century. They fasten together big sections that are carried into space aboard shuttles.

Mobile Foot Restraint (MFR)

jet backpack Manned Maneuvering Unit (MMU)

One of the hardest jobs they had was fixing the Hubble Space Telescope. First, the shuttle had to chase the telescope so the robotic arm could grab it. The arm was operated by an astronaut inside the shuttle. The arm slowly brought the telescope to the cargo area of the shuttle. Astronauts in space suits then lifted new parts and carefully put them in place. On Earth the parts were heavy. But in space they were weightless. If they had had to, the astronauts could have lifted the whole telescope, even though its weight on Earth is more than twelve tons.

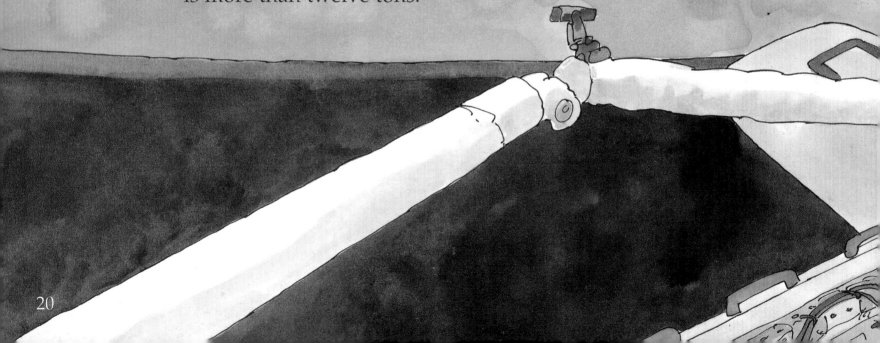

When the astronauts were finished, the telescope was put back into orbit. At all times during the repair, the telescope was held tightly. If it had been let go, the telescope might have floated away.

Outside the shuttle, astronauts must keep hold of everything. The object could be as small as a pin or big as a section of a space station. No matter the size, it would move forever unless something stopped it. Everything must be held—by strings, snaps, Velcro strips, or other fasteners.

An astronaut easily lifts a 600-pound replacement part for the Hubble telescope.

When astronauts are ready to sleep, they do not snuggle down into nice, cozy beds. Instead they get inside sleeping bags that may be hanging from a wall. The zipper is closed enough to keep an astronaut from floating free. An eyeshade

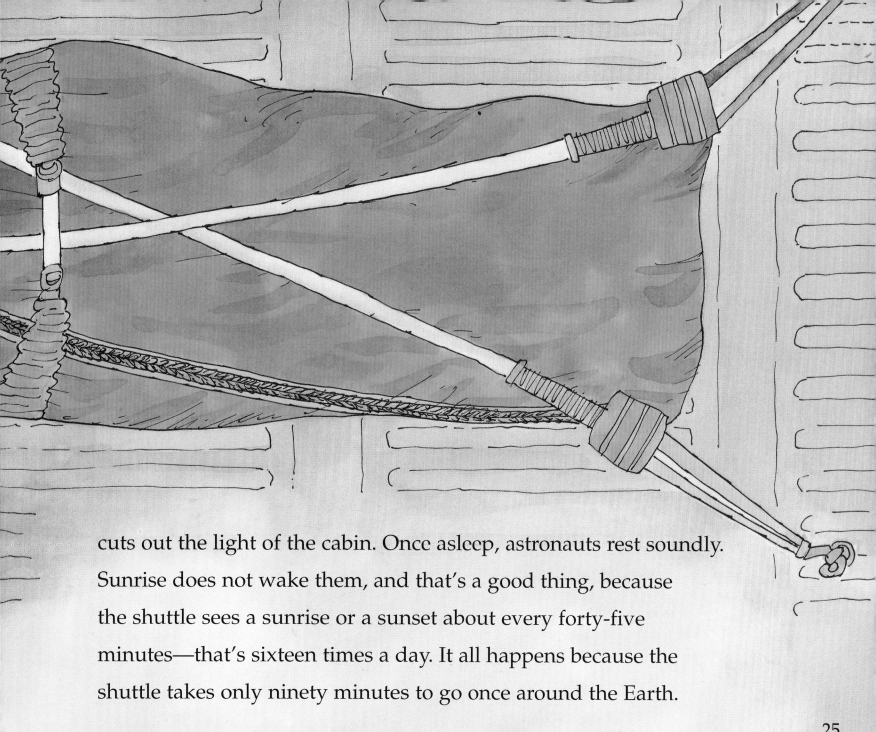

cuts out the light of the cabin. Once asleep, astronauts rest soundly. Sunrise does not wake them, and that's a good thing, because the shuttle sees a sunrise or a sunset about every forty-five minutes—that's sixteen times a day. It all happens because the shuttle takes only ninety minutes to go once around the Earth.

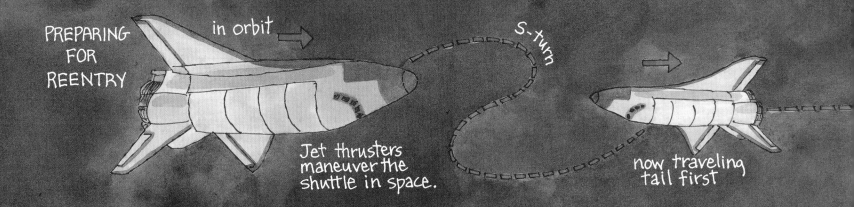

PREPARING FOR REENTRY

in orbit →

Jet thrusters maneuver the shuttle in space.

S-turn

now traveling tail first

After a few days the astronauts have completed their jobs and are ready to return to Earth. Everything is double-checked to be sure nothing can float free inside the cabin. The shuttle has been flying between two and three hundred miles above Earth, and it has been going 17,500 miles an hour. To drop out of orbit, the shuttle must slow down. The ship swings around and the engines fire backward. Once it has slowed down, the shuttle swings around so the nose is forward. The bottom of the ship is toward Earth, where it will remain.

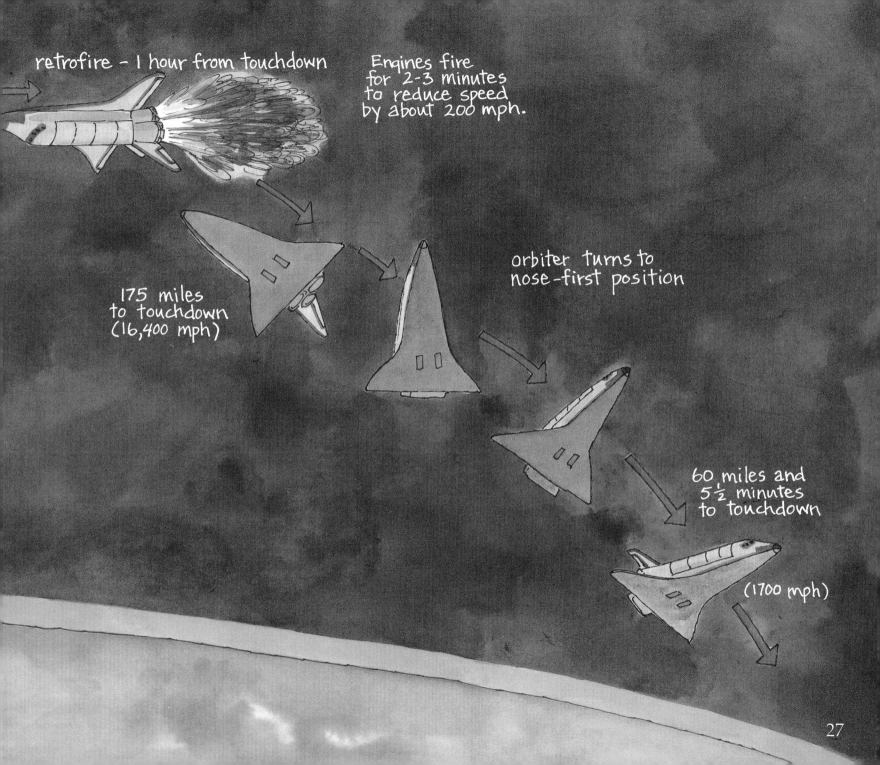

retrofire – 1 hour from touchdown

Engines fire for 2-3 minutes to reduce speed by about 200 mph.

175 miles to touchdown (16,400 mph)

orbiter turns to nose-first position

60 miles and 5½ minutes to touchdown

(1700 mph)

The shuttle eases in toward Earth.
Gradually, gravity increases. The
astronauts can feel it. The ship
slows down as it enters our
atmosphere. The shuttle becomes a
glider—an airplane without an engine.

As it speeds through Earth's atmosphere, the ship heats rapidly; parts of it get red-hot.

The shuttle comes down in a long, long glide. It gets closer and closer to Earth. At last the ship is a small dot that grows larger rapidly as it approaches the landing strip. Lightly and softly, the shuttle touches down.

chase plane

NASA
928

NASA

United States of America

The astronauts take a while to get used to gravity. Then they step out of their ship. Their mission is complete.